A Journey

of

Faith

An Autobiographical Narrative

Serville Waterman, PhD, DD

A JOURNEY OF FAITH
AN AUTOBIOGRAPHICAL NARRATIVE

Scripture quotations marked KJV are from the Holy Bible, King James Version (Authorized Version). First published in 1611. Quoted from the KJV Classic Reference Bible, Copyright © 1983 by The Zondervan Corporation.

iUniverse books may be ordered through booksellers or by contacting:

iUniverse
1663 Liberty Drive
Bloomington, IN 47403
www.iuniverse.com
844-349-9409

ISBN: 978-1-5320-9719-5 (sc)
ISBN: 978-1-5320-9721-8 (hc)
ISBN: 978-1-5320-9720-1 (e)

Library of Congress Control Number: 2021902692

Print information available on the last page.

iUniverse rev. date: 03/29/2021

Contents

While I live will I praise the Lord: I will sing praises
unto my God while I have my being.
-Psalm 146:2

This book is dedicated to the memory of my late mother Florence Waterman, affectionately known as Mother/Prophetess Waterman; and to all parents and guardians who have struggled with their children, and taught them to have faith in God.

A Journey of Faith

Serville Waterman is Pastor, Inventor, and Professor at the Brooklyn Theological School of Ministry and a practicing Christian.

His work at the school and as assistant pastor at the Hill of the Lord Ministry has touched thousands of lives.

Waterman has taught Theology at and Bible Studies in numerous churches in New York City for over 15 years. He has lived in Barbados, England, and the United States of America.

He attended and has earned several academic degrees:

He is an active prayer intercessor to many people all over the world and is knowledgeable in the fruits and gifts of the Holy Spirit.

Preface

My decision to write this book: *A Journey by Faith* was made several years ago while I was at low ebb in life. *It was the result of a challenging but memorable encounter that occurred during a worship service at one of the most popular churches in New York City.*

This book is about in no way meant to derogate, castrate, or embarrass anyone. It is my experiences which I would like to share. For too long Christians especially leaders have suffered in silence and not let others know that they are hurting. "If you cut us do we not bleed, if you hurt us do we not cry" This is my life story. I have lived it. I hope that, when I am through writing this book, I can put my demons to sleep. Don't judge me, or anyone for that matter. Instead, thank God that you have not walked in my shoes.

"Gifts are given to men without repentance" so says Corinthians, so I began to take my gifts seriously.

Acknowledgements

I am grateful for a large number of people, for help, inspiration, wisdom and encouragement in the preparation of this work. Many family members, friends, Christians, Jews, Muslims, Israelites, men and women I have met, have impressed upon me the importance of having and maintaining faith in God.

Sylvia Waterman, my life and work partner whose wisdom, ideals, support, and patience combine to propel the work I do, and to infuse enjoyment into every moment I am doing it.

Part One

Family

Although Barbados, which is often referred to as Little England; is not a big island, it is known for its beauty, mystique, and its unique location: 100 feet below sea level. It has luscious mountains, contrasting with steep green valleys, manicured farmlands surrounded by sandy beaches, where fishermen bring in their hauls of the famous flying fish. It seems to be a modern melting pot, with lots of tourists, and returning citizens vying for centre stage of fun in the sun. However, life on the island was sometimes quite different, interesting and even challenging decades ago. Along with its renowned reputation for high literacy rate, colonial style vestiges of politeness and diplomacy; there seems to be an indelible web of racism, classism and colour prejudice. The historical records bear proof. There were plantations, with great houses owned and operated by white folk, and staffed by light-skinned house maids, and dark skinned field workers.

I was born in 1945 to Westerman Nathaniel Waterman and Florence Waterman affectionately called Mother/Prophetess Waterman. I was eleventh in position of our middle-class Christian family of 13 children. Most of us were born at home and attended to by midwives, this was the norm in Barbados, in those days. Four siblings passed away in their infancy, as mother often mentioned. Large families were the order of the day, especially for Christian families. In those days, contemporary family planning methods and contraceptives were non-existent. People literally lived out the words of this popular Bible verse: *"Lo, children are a heritage of the LORD: and the fruit of the womb is his reward" (KJV- Psalm 127:3).*

There was always prayer, church hymns being hummed around the home. The six oldest brothers and sisters were sent off to the United States, Trinidad, and England (as was customary) for young adults to be sent to older relatives, to advance their education, and or make a decent living for themselves.

I grew up in Saint Andrew with my parents and two remaining siblings-a brother and sister. When we were off from school, and church, we all worked on our small family farm, taking care of the various cash crops, cows, goats, hogs, and fowls, which we reared for domestic use and community sale.

Some things can be very difficult for children to explain. However, I think children do know and feel a great deal about what has been happening around them; even if they cannot articulate an explanation of their feelings. As early as about 3 years old, I had begun to have visions of things to happen and things that were happening. When I told my mother, she would shut me up. I did not take it seriously at that time, and no one else did either. My path continued. Regardless!

When I was age 5, I was made aware that I am a black, a boy, with unique abilities. I also knew that some of my relatives and friends were given preferential treatment because of their light skin colour. I was called *Sammy Geese, because it was said that* I was the spitting image of a dark skinned man who was so named because of his colour. I can remember other dark-skinned 'Bajans' children being treated likewise. Nonetheless, my unique gifts continued, and I had a happy childhood, with lots of fun in *'Little England'*

Grand-Ma Mary

Mother often mentioned with pride that her mother, my maternal grandmother Mary Jordan, lived for many years in a great house on Farmers' Road in St. Thomas. She would also mention how it was always a treat when Grandma visited her every week. She wore beautiful floral dresses, stiffly starched and well ironed with equally pristine white-cotton apron. It had large pockets in which she brought letters sent from relatives abroad, photos, and money for us. She would always bring a large picnic basket full of delicious treats: pastry, jams, cured meat and other delicacies that mother could not afford on a regular basis.

As the years went by, Grandma Mary became old and frail. She moved from St. Thomas, and was living in a small house beside our home in St. Andrew. She spoke perfect English with a thin and stiff upper lip that seemed more starched than her apron. Mother was especially proud of her and grateful for all the help and family updates that from grandma. My siblings and I had to be on our Ps and Qs when she was around, but we loved her dearly.

My father was not always around, and I have no memory of my maternal grand-father or my paternal grandparents. They were born in the 18th C, and had expired before my entry on this planet. I gleaned from my parents' accounts, that my deceased grandparents were gentle folks, who worked hard to make a decent living for themselves. Our family farm was part of the land handed down from them. Sometimes, crops and animals were bartered for other products that mother needed, or sold for cash to people who vended in the markets. They would travel on trucks with their wares to the markets on Saturdays, the prime market day on the island.

It is amazing how so many things can happen in our lives. Things that we do not quite understand. Things that shape our beliefs and expectations that are intricately woven into myriad experiences that influence our destiny in life's journey.

Interestingly, I grew up seeing my mother being revered and held in awe as a prophetess. I could sense that the villagers were nervous when she came around them because they knew that all her prophesies negative or positive events were right on target. I was also aware that I could see and touch many things and beings looking like people, which no one else seemed to be able to see and or touch. I can vividly remember as early as 7 years of age, an array of unique childhood experiences that when shared, had earned me a multitude of nicknames: *Weird Geese, Psychic Boy, and Brainiack.*

Although I did not like any of those names, and could not get rid of them, I was enjoying the experiences of special visions, strange appearances, and uncanny occurrences in my childhood. I was happy because my siblings and peers could not fathom them. My mother thought they were peculiar traits and watched me with cautious apprehension. She told me to say the Lord's Prayer each time I encountered an angel or spirit. My six year old brain gradually got comfortable with the many unique encounters and I later learned to embrace them as a special gifting. I learned to pray, sing hymns, and to trust in God from my childhood.

Part Two

Father's Aroma
Visiting Spirit
Grandma's Journey

My father was a man of few wise words. He died peacefully in his bed in 1952. Weird things began to happen. I watched as my father's body was being prepared for burial. I still do not think that anyone knew that I was watching. The smell of perfume and powder filled his room. I went to pasture our sheep and cows, with my godfather David Best. There was always that smell of perfume and powder lingering around. The aroma followed me for years, all the way from my childhood days in Barbados to London England, a decade later. Every time, I smelt his burial fragrance, I would remember him from my seven year old boy memories.

Visiting Spirit

The potty was my constant companion as a wicked bout of diarrhea that invaded my stomach with relentless hurt. After the doctor's medicine showed no signs of relief, my mother fed me coconut water, and hard-dough bread soaked in ginger tea; but nothing seemed to work. I was ill for days, and prayers were being said for me around the clock. But mother could not take it anymore. She got dressed and said to my older brother *"When he dies come over to the church and get me"*. Then she left to the church which was across the street from our home.

I was lying on the bed, pleading with God for help so my stomach would stop hurting. Then, a wonderful and fantastic thing happened. Suddenly, I saw this beautiful middle-aged woman, with golden blonde hair, and beautiful kind eyes. I remember that her eyes were dark blue. She appeared in the doorway and came towards me. She laid her hands on my stomach and the pain left my stomach instantly. She then placed both her hands on my face and said to me, *"Son you will make me proud"*. The diarrhea disappeared and, I jumped off the bed to follow her.

When I got to the doorway of the bedroom, which led to the living room, she disappeared in thin air. One of my brothers who was in the living room at the time, looked up, saw me and said, *"Go back and lie down and die"*. I've never shared this information with him, nor my mother. They both have passed within the last 5 years.

Life has many mysteries in store for us from birth to eternity. Some are daunting, while others are complicated, and can take decades for us to connect the pieces of the puzzle, and enjoy the fullness of the picture.

This happened on a hot Wednesday in high school while I was on a break. My curiosity got the best of me. I took a penny and bridged it between two electrical wires that were exposed. I did not realize how dangerous this was because I knew nothing about the intricate details of electricity while growing up as a country boy. All I knew was to flip a switch and the light would go off and on. I could have died instantly, if the floor were wet. It was a miracle that I survived.

Apparition with the White Head Scarf

Another incident that I reflect on in High School was when I missed the school bus from Bridgetown to Saint Andrew, the village where I resided. I had to take the scheduled bus, which was over loaded due to the amount of the passengers sitting and standing. As if overcrowding were not enough of a challenge, the bus broke down and we had to disembark. A group of us began to walk towards the village, and then we saw a bus approaching. The bus made no attempt to stop. I began to run up the hilly road, thinking the bus would slow down. It did not. So, I ran to the valley road, where the bus' speed seemed safe for me to be able to jump on the bus.

When I jumped on the bus I missed the pole, and to my amazement my hands were caught in an old woman's head tie. It was white, and she was wearing a matching white dress. She looked at me as if to say *"why did you do that?"* I sat down beside the woman to thank her for saving my life. I felt such a sense of peace sitting near her. I arrived at my stop and I turned to thank her, but she had mysteriously disappeared. I pondered, and pondered before I decided to tell any of my friends. I did not wish to add to the growing list of nicknames they had been creating for me.

It is interesting to reflect how my older family members seemed always ready to meet death. It was approaching our family again, and my mother told me that I would have to stay with my grandmother. Grandma Mary had refused to eat, and she stayed in her bed because she knew that she was going to die. I kept her company by sleeping on the ottoman at nights.

One day she called me into her bedroom. She asked me to pull out the bottom drawer of her dresser. There was a very old white lace dress. It was probably made in 18th Century. There was an old stocking in the lace dress that was knotted. My grandmother asked me to undo the knot, and I did. To my surprise it was loaded with money. She said, *"Here, give this to your mother for the undertaker and my funeral. There should be some money left over".* Soon after, my grandmother Mary Jordan died peacefully at her home in St. Andrew Barbados, during summer vacation 1958.

My mother asked me to stay at home to watch the house while my grandmother's body was taken to the cemetery. I stayed in my grandmother's house and as I looked out the window I saw that neighbors had gathered around the house. I decided to play a prank on them. I took the white table cloth off the table and tied my head up. I slowly pushed my head up in the window. It was exciting to see grown men and women screaming and running in all directions from an imaginary ghost (duppy). I laughed so hard that I lost my grip and fell out the window. Naturally, when the elder women gathered themselves, they came back and complained to my mother about what I did. My mother told them that she could not give them any satisfaction, because they saw grandma's body being taken away and should not have let a 12 year old boy scare them half to death. *"It's your fault, not my son's fault"* she said. It made my day to have a healthy gut-busting laughter at those people, some of whom had been responsible for creating the unusual nicknames for me. Yippee! Yippee!

Life continued on the island as usual, and I grew as up as a teenager. I maintained an above average in my school work, and anticipated the day when I too would be sent off to England or America to join other relatives. I took a special interest in the family's mail delivery by our post man Mr. Ned. We got registered letter, parcels and telegrams with important messages. Our next door neighbor was quite nosey, and showed equally interest in seeing the type of mail that mom received. Every time money came from abroad for us, she would bring an item for sale to mother.

Mother would continue in grandma's footsteps by reading the letters from abroad, and providing delicacies for us. Sometimes the relatives overseas sent dollars and pound sterling from America and England respectively. All the money from relatives overseas came in handy to meet our living expenses. In my young mind, I could not understand why mother insisted on paying tithes (on tenth) of all the monies that came to her. I often wished she would give it to me so I could spend freely with my friends.

Part Three

Emigrating to England

I t was on a bright and sunny day in July, 1960, that my life began to take a new direction. I received a joint invitation letter from my brother and sister in England; telling me that they have paid for my air ticket to join them. At first glance of the letter, I could not believe that this was happening to me. I had just finished high school, and had had an earlier discussion with mother about my employment needs. I had asked if she would ask Mr. Brown to hire me as an apprentice to a Public Health Inspector. He was the Chief Health Inspector of my district in Saint Andrew, Barbados. My mother gave me a letter of introduction to take to Mr. Brown. I gave Mr. Brown the letter and was hired immediately. Mr. Brown had other health inspectors including a Mr. Scott, working at this office. One day, Mr. Scott gave me an errand to deliver a box of juicy fruit to a lady working at the church. I stopped off in a village near to mine, Saint Andrew, and entered the church. There I found the assistant organist named Sam. He seized the box and ate nearly all the fruit, leaving just a few which I took to the lady. I could discern that she felt insulted. That made the health inspector very angry with me; and he told me I could not be trusted. Sam, who ate the fruit and took advantage of my friendship, was married to my first cousin; I found that out later. So, the letter came just in time to relieve me of that embarrassing situation.

Barbados Exodus

My sister and brother sent me a suit, but it was too big.

My mother did not seem considerate enough to have the suit altered even though her brother was a tailor, and could have easily done this for me. I had to roll up the sleeves of the coat because they were too long. My day to leave the island finally came. Mother helped me prepare by doing my laundry. The clothes were not dry when I was ready to leave. So, she put the clothes in a plastic bag. When I got to the airport and went through customs the security guard said *"your clothes are wet"*. I explained that my mother packed them wet.

I was one of the first groups of people to fly to England by plane. Till then, everyone else had left by boat. All of us passengers boarded the British Airways plane at the Grantley Adams Airport in Barbados, West Indies.

The plane took off at 12:00 P.M. The arrival time was scheduled for 7:00 A.M. the following day to arrive at Idle Wile Airport, which is now called John F. Kennedy Airport (JFK) in New York, USA. (CHECK the TRAVEL TIME FOR ACCURACY) It was a regular stop over route for flights to England.

During an excited moment in my travel, I looked up and out from my window seat and noticed the plane engine was red as fire. I called to stewardess and told her that the engine was red. The stewardess said *"I am going to give you a job; I want you to keep an eye on the engine and tell me if it is not red."* I took my job seriously and watched to engine all nigh not knowing at the time that she was kidding me.

During that time I had a chance to reflect on multiple instances in my life, from when I was 3 years old until that time while I sat in the aircraft. I reflected on the nine children my parents had. All the boys slept in one bed. I was asleep on what looked like a huge pillow filled with grass on top of planks of wood. One of the planks shifted and I fell in the middle of the bed. No one could find me. Finally I wiggled free like a worm and was discovered by everyone. By all accounts of logic and reasoning, I should have been smothered. I began to remember my late dearly departed grandma Mary, my dad and his ever-present spiritual scent, my friends, Mom, and felt a tinge of loneliness for the first time. I was happy to be leaving the many nick-names behind as well.

I also pondered about one of my brothers who had relocated to the United States; and the other brother who had immigrated to the island of Trinidad. I guessed that I would not come to know them until much later in life.

Our airplane arrived at New York about 7.00 AM that morning, and all passengers had to disembark. We were escorted to a holding area. That was my first time on foreign soil, and life then felt a bit strange but positive.

It was 8:35 in the morning. I boarded the plane at Idlewyle Airport, now known as JFK, for the long journey to England. It took all day and the stewardess put me back in my seat and said, *"Remember your job, you have to watch that engine for me."* At around 7:30 she brought us dinner and told us we would be landing at Gatwick Airport at 10:30 P.M., London time.

On arrival, it was time to go through English customs. You should have seen the look on the immigration officer's face when I opened my tiny suitcase with a bag full of wet clothes. She asked me *"Did you go swimming?"* With a big smile on my face I said "I knew we were flying too close to the water." I did not knowing that the British Officer did not appreciate my wry humor. *"Why are your clothes wet?"* she said sternly. I told the officer it was raining in Barbados. My mother put my clothes out to dry but they got rained on, so she packed them wet. The officer replied, *"Try to get them dry before you put them on. I don't want you to be sick in England."*

I was so happy when I recognized my two brothers waiting for me at the arrival gate. They hurriedly took my small suitcase and they took me to the car to go to my sister's house. I didn't realize at the time that their haste was because they did not want me to be seen because I had on a suit that was two sizes too big. They were glad to see me although they were embarrassed. The car stopped in front of my sister's house and I went in. My brother, who is 3 years older than I, found me some clothes that really fit. Although it was August, they had a coal fire going and I promptly got in front of the fire to keep warm. There was a knock on the door. It was my brother who migrated to Trinidad and whom I would be meeting for the first time. He had immigrated to Trinidad 23 years before when I was born.

He asked my family, "Who is this young man. My sister asked *"who does he look like?"* He replied *"He looks like us."* My sister said, *"Fool; that is your last brother, Serville."* That was when I finally met this brother who had lived in Trinidad for decades, before I arrived in England at the age of sixteen. Here we were together on my first day in England. I was very happy for the new environment and family connections.

Getting Busy for Progress

By the second day, it was time for me to look for a job. I went out to check the factories and offices that had **'HELP WANTED'** signs postings. At one of the offices I was interviewed by a manager, and he hired me. It was a small company selling metal clamps. My English was very good, so the boss of the company sent me to Waterloo Station. I gave the taxi driver a 5 pound tip not knowing that would be my salary per week. He responded *"Thank you Governor."* When I told my boss, he became agitated and fired me on the spot. Now I was looking for another job.

My second job was with a company that made fur coats, and operated by a Jewish family. I was hired as a sweeper. At the end of the day I would sweep and match fur tails.

One day the boss was watching and, he commended me for the way I matched the furs.

The boss said, *"You come here, did you match this fur?* I said *"Yes"*. My boss said *"You have a good eye; I don't want you to sweep anymore. Go downstairs and work matching furs."* Unfortunately, my supervisor downstairs became envious of me. He would pass me pieces that he knew did not match. I became adamant and told him those were no matches. The owner of the company, who was secretly watching, told my supervisor that he would fire him if I had had at least six months more experience. The owner said to me that being a professional fur grader is like a gift. However, the Jewish boss did not reveal to me the true benefits. If I had known, I would have stayed and become a rich man in the fur trades, today. In the evenings after work, I attended academic classes for new immigrants. Our professor said we were the brightest students of the winter semester. I remember this vividly, with a keen sense of 'Bajan pride'. After the orientation session of expectation and responsibilities in English studies, our Professor, asked the students to discuss one word for 30 minutes. He said that he would not ask us to do anything he couldn't do. The Professor chose a 'door knob' as his topic. He talked for 30 minutes about the door knob. I was so impressed. He did not divert from his topic. I have since learned how to choose one word and talk about it for half hour. It was an amazing experience in focus skills, which I still find helpful today.

I kept applying for other jobs and was very excited and elated when I received my letter to work for the Internal Revenue. I was to begin working in the Title Redemption Department. My job was to restore maps, before they were given to the draftsman. The restorations enabled them to know landmass, oceans, boundaries, and where to find them on the map. Technology was coming and we were gearing up to store on microfiche films. There were no computers at that time. I shared an office with an English guy, who from day one on the job, had tried to sabotage me. He tried to craft a malicious way for the supervisors to get rid of me. Like a friendly devil, he said *"you can tell me your secrets"*. He asked *"have you ever been in prison or reform school?"* I explained to him, *"If I had had any record of being arrested or had a mental problem I would have been denied a Passport"*. His reason for asking was based on systemic racism: Because I am/was black he had thought with prejudice that I had to have some kind of criminal record. As far as the world and I know, criminal activities affect all groups of people regardless of ethnicity, creed, or gender. Sadly, many other racists behave the same way today. A sad reality!

I attended Kingsway College three days a week because of my educational background, and worked for two days a week. That is when I met trouble. I met a guy at school who was studying French and English Literature. He had a fantastic proposition. He asked me to tutor his sister in Mathematics and English. He said that he could not feed me; and instead, he offered me room and board. This sounded good to me, especially because I was not satisfied with my sister's treatment of me at that time.

I was living in my sister's house, paying rent and for my own food. My sister had a young daughter who suffered from respiratory problems. The doctor would sometimes make emergency visits between the hours of 2-3 AM, several mornings per week. It was a family challenge for all of us. Unfortunately, my sister never considered that it was wrong and unfair to send me to the pharmacy at that time of the morning to pick up my niece's medicine. I had no complaint until I found out how dangerous such errands were. I met another immigrant who schooled me. He told me the Teddy Boys gang would kill immigrants who they found walking alone at night. I moved out of my sister's house that same day.

After I moved I began to tutor this young woman. Initially we were chaperoned. It was soon after that her mother went off to have a relationship with someone else, so we were no longer chaperoned. We became intimate. Things did not last and we went our separate ways.

I left the Internal Revenue Service, where I had been working as a Junior Officer. I enlisted in the Royal Air Force, and I was accepted as an airman. I got in the plane and showed how competent I was at flying. The instructor said, *"Now land"*. I looked at him and replied, *"You land it. I am the student"*. I passed the test and became an Air Force Instructor for the Air Training Corps (ATC), which is equivalent to American ROTC.

I was flight instructor for the ATC No. 305 (Ashford) Squadron, (Kent). After a while, I left the Air Force for civilian life. I searched everyday for a job but, was always told, I was over qualified. I went to a vocational training school in Croydon. I had to travel by bus five days a week. I trained to be a silk screen printer.

The very week that I received the first pay check in my life in England, my workmate took me to what would be equivalent to a check cashing store, for me to change my check. His other motive was because he wanted me to participate in football pools-gambling. He told me all that I needed to do was to mark 8 Xs on the form and it would cost me 3 shillings and 9 pence. I did as he instructed and I was all ready to submit it when I noticed that his had 18 X's for 2 shillings and 6 pence. I questioned him. But not getting the full understanding, I told him that I wanted to play it the same way that he did. Had I left it as it was, I would have won 75,000 pounds in 1960. That would have been equivalent to $30 million USA at that time.

VISIONS

Let me start by saying, I am not demented. I have never been on any type of psychological drugs. I was on no medication and, I was not hallucinating.

I had decided to go for a walk. I left the campus feeling good. I was walking along a two hedged road. My heart began to race. I felt in my soul that I had been here before. The environment seemed familiar. I looked up and there was the figure of an elderly white man walking towards me. I asked him, "Where is the airfield around here. He took off his hat, scratched his head, and he answered: *"You mean the airfield for the Yanks? Go up the hill and you will see a pub. The yanks airfield is behind the pub?* I went up the hill. I was extremely surprised when I got to the top of the hill. I discovered a very old airfield. It was where 'Yanks' took off and landed airplanes in World War 1. Immediately, I knew who I was in a previous life. I knew what I did and, why I was there. It all came back to me, flooding my memories, and my inner being. That convinced me that there are many intricate weaves to my life and human life in general. Life in England was taking on new meanings to me as well.

On another occasion as I can remember, I was relaxing on my sofa, staring at the wall. Suddenly, two white men emerged from the wall. They were dressed in military uniforms. I felt an empty feeling in my stomach that slowly began to fill up. My instincts told me one of those men was me.

At another time I was lying in bed, staring at the ceiling. Suddenly, I felt as if I were out of my body. I was on the ceiling, and was actually staring down at myself. The image slowly floated down towards me. Then there was a thud, as if I had gone back into myself. I felt a spiritual clarity after this experience. It made me never afraid to die, or take chances.

Yet another curious experience! One evening while coming home from work, I saw the two boys and, when they saw me their heads were resting on the broken glass of the window. I had to do some quick thinking. I told the boys, *"Let's play a game. Whoever can stay very still until uncle gets in the house will get ice cream."* They remained still. I got the kids out of the window and took them for ice cream.

Another Dream and Vision

One night I had another special this dream. I dreamt that there was a man on a donkey's carriage. The man beckoned to me to get on the cart. I climbed up on the cart, and I sat with him all night, while he rode around. Finally he stopped, right on top of a bridge. He motioned for me to get off the cart.

Three days later, I received a letter and a ticket to go to Ashford Kent for a new job. I got off the express train at Ashford. I asked someone how to get to the industrial area where the jobs were. The station master directed me to go on top of the bridge to catch the bus to the industrial estate. I went to the top of the bridge and I suddenly realized it was the same bridge I had been on, in my dream 3 nights before.

Blessings began to flow. After three months on the job, I got the shock of my life. I was hired in Ashford Kent. The personnel office called me. I was given the key to a brand new house. I was told to go get my family.

Intuition in Gambling and Buying a Car

I went to a very timely poker game, with a union representative from my job. The players thought I was a pigeon. A pigeon is one considered to be someone who they could easily take money from. I lost 25 pounds sterling initially, but then, I was dealt four aces and, I won 300 pounds sterling. A young man with whom I worked loaned me the rest of the money so that I was able to buy myself a car. I was set for a little while.

My next agenda was to become adept at driving. I failed the test in London. I took lessons from a local guy, who was an ex-racing car driver. My next door neighbour, who was of gypsy culture, hit me in the back with a shoe the day of the exam. I thought she was crazy. She explained *'"That's our way of saying good luck."* I knew I had to pass that test, because I did not want her to hit me again. The instructor said, *"Good Luck. You are the most competent student that I have had. It was a privilege to test you."* I then had my driver's license. Hooray!

I proudly drove my car to work the next day. My supervisor, whom I will refer to as Matt, immediately became envious of me. He was angry. He had not been successful in passing his driver's test. Matt's wife worked in the evening. We greeted each other, as we usual, but Matt became belligerent. He told his wife, *"If I ever catch you in that man's car, I will kick your ass."* I was shocked. I said, *"What did I do to you."* The union representative said: *"You have your license, you are showing him up. He is acting that way because of the car. He can't pass the driver's test."*

The French Experience

This is another strange but true experience. A few Saturdays after, I worked until midday, and came home for lunch. Lunch was not ready; so I turned on the television while lunch was being prepared. There was a French movie, with English sub-titles. I felt tired so I turned off the television and, I went to sleep. Suddenly, while I was sleeping, I saw a tall thin white man. He was with a French girl. They were walking in a meadow; talking, laughing, and holding hands. I got the shock of my life when I realized that tall thin white man was me -Serville Waterman! That was the same man I saw in my vision three years ago. I panicked and

I tried to wake myself up. I could not so, I panicked more. The white, French woman began to patting me on my back saying "Ne t'en fais pas. Tu es bien. Mon Cheri. Ne t'inquietes pas. Tu es bien. Mon Cheri." *"Don't worry, don't worry my dear, you will be all right, you will be all right, everything will be all right."*

I thought. But, I am black, these people are white. My heart began to race. I jumped up speaking French which I had never learnt before. I do not know how many of you out there can relate to any of my experiences. But I am convinced that I was here on earth in another life, and time. Glory to God!

My First Visit to America

I came to America in 1973 to visit my family. My grandfather, whom I never met, had passed away in 1971. I thought it would be good to see my grandmother, not realizing my grandmother was my grandfather's third or fourth wife.

I thought of immigrating to the US for a fresh start in 1973. I was happy to have my other brother who had been in the USA before I was born. I was 34 yrs old, when I myself came to the United States.

I spent time with my brother, who is now an Arch-Bishop in Canada. America was a new and exciting experience to me. I met my baby sister. She tried to convince me to stay. However, I needed to go back to England to tie up some loose ends and finalize my departure in a proper way. England has been home to me and with many interesting experiences for so many years. I needed a nice closure. On my return to England, I remained in Ashford.

I changed jobs. I was a civilian employee for the Ashford Police Station. My faith was rekindled. I had a good friend from Jamaica West Indies and we would go out to parties and visit each other. I had to prove something to myself. I knew God was never to be feared, but to be loved.

How God was Revered in Barbados

In Barbados, West Indies we were taught that God was such a cruel and fearful God. At age 13, we had an American Evangelist came to our small church and he preached hell fire, brimstone, and that God was an angry God of damnation; with a big stick looking for you to do something wrong. We youngsters got saved every night. We went to the Alter and repented what we did not do. I thank God that my mother made us memorize scriptures. I memorized John 3:16.

God's Presence with Me in England Too

Later in England, as miracles continued to unfold in my life, I told my friend, *"We have to go to church"* My Jamaican friend and I went to church. I rededicated my life to God. I was so into religion by works. I sold my records, including my collection of Jazz R & B, Classical Music. I stopped drinking beer. I disassociated myself from my old friends. My friend and I began, to look to God. God loves me and he brought me through hell. When I think about how God had protected me, I realize that he is a loving and forgiving God. God Almighty is the God of second chances, and Life Eternal!

One Saturday night I loaned my mega speakers to some of my neighbors, who lived a mile and a half away. They were calling me. I was compelled to go. *I wore* my blue satin shirt, with an oversized collar, dark blue velvet pants, and platform shoes. At that time I had no driver's license. I had to get home before the local police pulled me over. This car was one of the cars I had before I won the jack pot from my friends at work. The car had four different wheels. Each wheel was different. Two tires blew up as I was going at 85 MPH. Two tires bust and the car was headed 85 miles per hour into a brick wall. I said, *"I'm not going to die tonight."* I turned the steering wheel away from the wall and, I jammed my hand there so that it wouldn't turn back to the wall. It hit the rail and, bounced back three times then, flipped over. My good friend could not believe what he had just seen. He looked at the condition of the wrecked car. The car was flat. He backed away. I asked him *"What is wrong brother?"* I grabbed him. *"Let me go, please!"* he said, *"Are you alive, there is no way you got out of that car alive. The doors are sealed shut and smashed in".* The car was towed and junked. He went home to get his car. I realize that God saved my life. I was not about to leave God, again. He is merciful and will send angels to help you and me.

Saved From A Terrible Accident

Another miracle happened on a rainy morning, while I was on my way to work. The roads were slippery, and I was speeding. I did not want to be late for work. I noticed a car crossed ways in the road. The car was not moving and, blocking my path. I applied the brakes, and the car began to go toward some houses which were below the road. My car was stick shift driven. I tried to change gears, but it only went to third gear. I tried hard to take it to fourth gear. I saw the driver of the other car bracing for impact. His hands were over his face, with his arms in a crisis-crossed position. I felt like someone had taken hold of my hands off the steering wheel. My car turned on a right angle, never hitting him. Again, I felt as if someone literally put my hands back on the wheel. I continued to drive to work. I was in amazement. I told my mechanics and my co-workers about this awesome incident. They said it happened because I am an advanced driver. I told them it was a miracle. One of the young men told me to kneel down to a pile of bricks. He said: *"There is no God".* I looked him dead in his eyes and said, "You would not say that if you just experienced what I did." One day, I trust you will come to know Him.

Jealous Co-Worker

Within six months of working for the Ashford Police Department, I had problems with a certain civilian driver. He made it clear to me and everyone else, that he wanted my job. My co-workers laughed at him. They knew I was experienced, and they knew what my job entailed. I had to order gas for a 300 gallon tank. All orders and measurements had to be precise. You could be fired for ordering too little or, too much gas. I had to keep stock and inventory of tires, engine parts, and, electrical parts. Also, I had to manage accounts for three other Police stations, one each in Rochester, Dover and Liddee. I had to know how to juggle motorcycles and their parts. I balanced accounts receivable and accounts payable. I did the audit check for vehicles and motorcycles. There were police vehicles that had 200,000 to 300,000 miles on them. They had to be stripped of all police markings, and driven to headquarters for auction. I was responsible for that. Quite frankly, I was the store man, accountant, and auditor. The workshop officer could not believe that I could balance the monthly audit book in twenty minutes. He said, *"You're the man I'm looking for. I will train you to do the rest of the job"*. We had a wonderful working relationship for three years.

Unfortunately, the certain civilian driver became jealous and vindictive. Reportedly, he took off my gas tank. My car was in a police lot and, he was an employee. I complained to the detectives. However, they did nothing. One Friday night the trouble-maker came in singing: *"Somebody's car is going to blow up"*. I did not take notice. I drove my car home. I smelled gas, but I did nothing. A visitor from my church came by to see me. He was a kind and gentle, elderly white man. I asked him how he was getting home. He said that he was walking, so I offered to drive him home. We got in the car and there was still a very strong smell of gas. I thought then and there, I must ask my Jamaican friend to come to take a look at it. He came right away. He opened up the hood of my car. He said, *"I've never seen anything like this. The gasoline was boiling on top of the engine like water"*. The mechanic said, *"Go, hurry and get some rags to soak up the gas."* It was a V-8 engine. That is why the gas collected. It seemed that someone had pulled off the return hose from the carburetor. The gas was being pumped onto the engine.

We have had no explanation why my car did not blow up. My friend put the hose back on the carburetor and put on an alligator clip. This made it difficult to be removed without tools.

The following Monday morning I went to work. I noticed that my co-workers were looking at me in a questionably funny way. So, I said: *"What's happening?"* They responded, *"As if you don't know?"* I said, *"know what?"* The driver who kept harassing me for my job almost died. His car blew up. The police just got him out in time, before his car exploded. They accused me jokingly, of working some kind of Voodoo. I said, *"No please! God takes care of his own."* They really believed that I had some supernatural powers, or knew how to work Voodoo. This frightened them. They never bothered me anymore and were always polite.

Prejudice on the Job

One day, two undercover police officers came to the Ashford Station. I was standing near the door. They asked me for the workshop manager, not knowing that I was he. I sent them to the office to wait for me, but I walked behind him. They were arrogant. The officers asked me "Where do you think you are going." One of the workers said to them: *"He is the Work-shop Manager."* They apologized, and began to call me 'Sir'. They told me what they wanted. I told them that I did not have it, but could send a mechanic to town, to fetch the items for them. *"He will go to a dealer and, get you four new tires".* The officers were surprised, and impressed, that a black man, of competence was holding that position.

Welcome to America

I decided to go back to America for a fresh start. It was the year, 1976. My relatives were who were all settled there, decided to help me as best as they could. At least, so I thought. After searching around, I found a room for rent, opposite my sister's house.

My land lord was an avid gambler. He would ask me for a dollar everyday to play numbers. I asked him how I would ever know if and when I won. He told me that I should look in the newspapers; for the number that played for the racetrack it would be the last three numbers. When I won, he told me that I had it wrong it was the first three numbers. That went on for a while with him changing from the last three to the first, and vice versa. Three times when I thought that I had won, he played me a 6 for a 9. I decided that I would no longer play because of his dishonest behavior. So, he decided to kick me out as his tenant. I was happy to leave non-the-less, and so I found an apartment at a different location.

Having My Own Apartment

When I got the apartment, I did not have enough money to pay for a truck, so my relatives and I pushed the bed for two blocks. You could not imagine the laughter coming from my sister and family, as they looked over their veranda. It was funny to me too, in retrospect.

Dumplings and Domino Game

One day my mother cooked some dumplings, and she brought me some. She had not known that my brother-in-law (sister's husband) had counted them before she brought me some. It was when I went over to play a game of dominos that he told me that he had counted the dumplings and that five of them were missing. It was an embarrassing occasion, but my brother and I decided to get back at him by beating him severely in the game of dominos. No harm, all was fun.

Ignorance is No Bliss

Sometimes we as new immigrants can become so overwhelmed with excitement and the newness of life that we often go around without knowing the basics of life in a new environment. Anybody out there knows what I am speaking about?

My case in point was that I had no idea, that coming from England in those days, I had permission to work stamped in my passport. I honestly did not know that I could apply for jobs relating to my wealth of experience and would provide me with better opportunities. So, I worked at menial tasks, such as bus boy and pot washer to make a living.

To demonstrate how ignorance can be a disadvantage, I have to tell you about an experience I had when I worked in Manhattan at a pub. An inspector came in and said that there was so much filth on the floor, and it had to be removed. The owner offered the job to someone else for $25 and he refused. He then offered it to me and additional $10 and I agreed. I felt so desperate for work and money to take care of my responsibilities. I got down on the floor and scrubbed it clean. I removed 36 bags of filth from the floor. When I was finished he gave me a pint of Guinness and $35 and told me to get out of his pub because I stink. Can you imagine that?

Not smelling myself, and having no idea how bad the odour was, I took the train to 42nd Sreet. When the door opened the people rushed in, and hastily rushed back out again. Every time the train stopped the same thing would happen and I was left to ride alone in the car until I reached Utica where I got off.

In order for me to get on the bus, I kept the token in my hand and put it in quickly. The bus driver told me that I could not get on. I told him my money was already in. He then told me to go to the back because I stink. On the bus the same thing happened as on the train, everyone coming on changed their minds and went back off.

When I came off the bus I walked towards my house and rang the bell in my special way to let them know that I was home. My family opened the door and slammed it shut before I could say a word. They opened it again after a while and handed me a garbage bag with the order to strip! I took off everything and put them in the bag then I had to take about 12 showers before I smell better. I had used up about 2 bottles of shampoo and a whole bar of soap. In the end it cost me more doing that job than it was worth. Yuck! Ignorance really stinks, and it can be very expensive.

Another time when I worked at another restaurant, I observed that the cook had asked two male workers to bring him some flour and salt. Surprisingly, they came back with sugar and eggs. He yelled at them and then turned to me and asked if I could get him the correct things. I willingly got him the correct items, flour and salt. Later, I asked the guys why they had brought the wrong things, because obviously they knew what he was asking for. It was then that I learnt that they wanted to work delivering food because they would get tips that would amount to hundreds of dollars when the week was up. From then I too misunderstood what the cook asked for and so I was able to work delivery and get some tips myself. Because of my English accent I got even more than the other workers and so I was stopped from delivering on a Fridays, and was asked to clean the stoves. I did such a good job that *I* was given the leftover food to take home. All in all, it was worth much more to me this way than to be working with the cook.

After about three years of survival jobs, I was able to sponsor myself with the degree which I had, and then I began applying for and obtaining better jobs

Snatched Baby Carriage from Subway Tracks

One day while I was on the train, a woman opened the carriage door screaming her head off. The conductor asked what the matter was. She motioned towards the end of the carriage, stating very frantically that her baby was between two subway cars. What we later learnt was that the baby carriage had slipped down while she was transferring from one car to the other. At this time sparks was flying from the baby's carriage that was scraping on the ground between the cars. The conductor said that there was nothing he could do. I, without thinking pulled the emergency brakes, opened the door and when the train stopped, I stretched out my hands holding onto the baby carriage and lifting it out of harm's way, giving it to the mother who was very grateful and thankful. The conductor was alarmed because he said that I could have been electrocuted. I guess that God was protecting me that day. I could have even lost my hands when the cars snapped back together.

A Bold Thief

I had drilled two holes and placed some nails to make it impossible for anyone to open the window from the outside. Now, this guy who was a bold thief had apparently tried opening the window without success, he was determine to get in the house, he was trying to get at it from the inside by removing the nails. When I called the police, the policeman told me to get some more nails to replace those that the thief took out, his parting words to me were *"Welcome to America, Mr. Waterman."*

The 'Blind' Man Beggar

A neighbor and I would usually travel to work together via the train. One day after stopping off to have a drink, as he usually did before he went to work; we were approached by a man wearing dark glasses, and was shuffling around while begging for handouts. I put my hand in my pocket and took out a dollar and was just about to place it in his hands when my friend slapped my hand away. I asked why he did that and he told me to wait a bit and I would see. Before we could reach the top of the stairs, the shuffling beggar came running past us with his dark glasses hanging on his shirt, open proof that he was not a blind man. Not only was he not blind, but he was very agile, and may have been stronger than I was.

Escape From Danger

I worked with an Italian food testing company for the lunch program that was organized by the mayor at that time. I had to test milk to ensure that it did not go sour, orange juice to ensure that it was not too acidic, and things of that nature. One day when we were making sandwiches to deliver to children in the black neighborhoods, I noticed that the salami was filled with greenish spots. I told the boss about it; alerting him that it would cause sickness if it were to be eaten by the children. He told me not to worry about it and that I should continue to send it to the assembly line to make the sandwiches. I refused. I was confronted by a supervisor who told me to do as I pleased. I went into the refrigerator and continued to work until it was time to go home. When I got to the door, I realized that I had been locked in. I banged on the door until my fingers were bloody. I was scared that I would freeze to death if I had to stay there over the weekend, because it was a Friday evening and the place would not be opened until Monday morning. You could imagine my horror. I heard someone scream at the top of his voice, *"If you don't let that man out I'm calling the police."* At that point I had been banging on the door for about 2 ½ hours.

Sometime later someone opened the door and asked me if I had learnt my lesson. I said "Yes". He then took me to his office and asked me to teach another guy whom I met there, all that I knew. I did that. He then asked me to go with him to the office. At this point my heart was racing, for I was trying to understand why he had asked me to teach another person on the spot after locking me in the freezer and now he was taking me to his office. I was scared. He asked the guy if I had taught him everything and when he said yes he gave me some money. According to him, some for me and some for my family. Then he warned me to keep my mouth shut and dismissed me. I began to run from that building, I ran past the train station, and past another and another, I was afraid to stop, even to catch the train. It was only when I was very far away from that place and comfortable enough, I went into the train station to take the train home.

From that time on, and possibly for about 2 years, I was scared when riding the train. I would have flash backs of that day. Sometimes I would get off the train before I got to my destination because of panic attacks.

There was a family emergency that needed cash. I withdrew $300 and took it to a real estate broker, and told him my predicament. He took me to this Jewish lawyer who ran a travel agency off Bergen and Flatbush.

When I got there, I handed the $300 over to the lawyer, who proceeded to count it. He went 20, 40,60, 80,100,120,140,160,180,200 and so on until he counted $400 and handed me back $100. He did this again, and got $400 again, and handed me back $100. This happened for a third time, and again he got $400, and handed me back $100. At this point in time here I am wondering what in the world had happened. Here I was on my last $300, I paid for the tickets, the man got his money, and I still had $300 left. But it did not end there.

The following day family members and I went to the airport. We were not aware that she needed her passport as well as the green card to travel. They were locked in a bank vault in Manhattan for safe-keeping.

This meant that we would have to go back for it, but time was against us. I decided to go in faith. I saw a Yellow Cab and I explained to the driver what the situation was. He agreed to take me to the bank on Chambers St., Manhattan to retrieve it for a fee of $100. When we got there it was 8.40 am. I knocked on the door and the guard came to my assistance. I explained what had happened and he went to call the manager. The manager, told me that the vault was on a time clock and would not open until 9.00 am. So I sat in the taxi until 9.00 am waiting for the bank to open.

When we retrieved the passport, I noticed that the clock said 9.10 am. The flight would start boarding at 9.15 am. I had exactly 5 minutes to get there. However the journey would take about one hour by the usual standards. I got into the taxi and we left. I was talking to my nephew, and the taxi driver spoke to me at that time, saying, "Sir, we *should not be here as yet.*" I told him to continue on, but he said to me again, "Sir we *should not be here as yet.*" It happened a third time that he said these words to me. When we arrived at the airport, the clock was saying 9.15am. I was amazed! I had hoped for a miracle, but did not expect anything as this. The booking agent said *"You guys must have just been to Brooklyn and back."* I said *"No we went to Manhattan."* He said *""N.! Not even a helicopter would have been able to make that trip so fast."* When I think about it, not even if we had gone to Brooklyn would we have made it in that time. I turned to the driver who began to back away from me as though I was a ghost. He did this until he reached the sliding door and began to run away from me. I was trying to pay him his $100 but he did not stop to get it. He just ran away as though I was a ghost. I could imagine what his thoughts would have been at that time. That day may have been a day of miracles.

Buying a House

Being an ardent Christian at that time, I fasted every Saturday and would break my fasting in the evening. I was sitting at the table, when I heard in an audible voice. *"Serville, Serville, Serville,"* I answered *"Yes."* Then I heard, *"I am going to give you a house"* I turned to my family members and asked them: *"Did you hear that?"* And they said *"Yes!"* and repeated exactly the same thing that I had heard. I was so dumb stricken, then I decided to walk up the block to the corner of Church Avenue, in Brooklyn. When I got there, I met a Real Estate Broker, who called me over and said to me. *"Excuse me Reverend, do you want to buy my house?"* I responded *"Yes."* He then told me to come in on my way from work on Friday afternoon and leave some money with him. At that time I was not a Reverend. It was only two years later that I was ordained as a minister.

I had no money at the time. I did not expect to be able to buy a house, but I believed that I had heard God's voice and therefore I should be obedient. All I could afford to give him at the time was $25 or $30 per week. Within a month he told me that since I had given him $1,000 which I had not, that we would be able to work something out.

The day came when we went in for closing. His lawyer asked for $5,000 to close. I told him that I had no money. The house owner got up to leave, but his lawyer asked that he hold on a little. He then said, *"Give the Reverend the keys, for I would be doing your taxes for you, and you would come off like a bandit."* The owner then threw the keys across the table, and I grabbed them and said *"Thank you Jesus!"* I left the closing as a homeowner without paying a dime more.

The broker drove us over to the house and explained that it was well furnished so we would not have to worry about furnishing. When we got to the house we could not move in because we had no money for a truck. Then a strange thing happened. A young man with a van came to visit me. Up to this day I don't know why he came, but he was there. I asked him if he could take my things to the house and he said *"sure thing"*.

We loaded up our clothes and put them into the truck and threw out the old bed. Now we were on our way to our new house. Our former landlord, observing us putting out the bed, laughed together with her sister.

After unloading our clothes and personal items from the truck, we went inside. In the kitchen I heard a hissing noise, and realized that it came from the pipe under the sink. I checked and the pipe was leaking. I knew that I would have to get this fixed as soon as possible but I had no money. I felt confused and hopeless, but I went outside and saw two gentlemen dressed with jackets and I approached them to see what help I could get. I told them what had happened and that I had no money. They immediately turned and came into the house to see the problem. When they saw what it was, they took off their jackets, place them on the table and proceeded to fix the problem. One of them, who lived nearby went to his home and came back with the necessary tools. When they were finished, I thanked them and told them that I did not know how to repay them. They said that I could not. I later learnt that one of them was a multimillionaire, who owned quite a few homes on the block, while the other gentleman worked for the United Nations. I pray every night that God would bless these men and their children.

Our former landlord who laughed at us on our departure went to my church, and on the following Sunday morning they told the pastor that I had gotten a new apartment. The pastor later asked me how I liked my new place. I told him that I had some problems with the thermostat. He told me that I should not touch it, that I should get the landlord to check it. I told him that I was the landlord. His response was *"What!"* Then he took off to the basement. I walked to the basement behind him, and overheard him castigating me, about where I got the money from and other things which I would not mention. They looked around and saw me and were so ashamed that they bent their heads and walked out.

When I got the house, it came with a small mortgage. After about two months paying our mortgage on time, there was less money coming in. I was unable to pay the mortgage by myself, so I got a delinquent notice in the mail for the first month. The second month, to my amazement, I received a letter from the mortgage company stating that after checking the escrow account, they found that I had overpaid and after deducting one month's payment they were now sending me a check for the sum of $67.

At this point I stood on the steps of my home with my hands lifted to the Lord praising and thanking him for his deliverance.

That could not have been a coincidence, but the spirit of God working. I prayed all the way to work that morning. At that time *I* worked at a local hospital, and while I was walking to my office, I found the ID card of the Chief Nursing Supervisor. I called her office and made arrangements to hand deliver it back to her at the lunch interval.

When I got to the office of the Chief Nursing Supervisor, the secretary wanted to take the ID from me but I told her that I was to give it to her personally. She reported this to the Supervisor who asked that I be sent in.

The supervisor was impressed and gave my relative an opportunity of gainful employment. I don't need to tell you that I no longer had trouble paying my mortgage. Thank God! While I was working as a Lab assistant for the Carbon Place, and was paying the owner of the house I was going to buy, I decided to buy myself a snow shovel. I wanted to show my belief in what God had spoken to me. One of my workmates asked me why I had bought the shovel and I told him that I was going to buy a house. The man fell on the floor with laughter, put his two feet in the air and tears were flowing from his eyes. He knew what my salary was and he found it unbelievable that I would be having this plan.

As he lay there, ridiculing me I heard the voice of God say *"Tell that fool that he would be living beside you within six months."* When I told him he fell on the floor laughing even louder. As it turned out my neighbor was moving to Florida and wanted someone to buy her house and I put the idea to his wife and she accepted and he really became my next door neighbor.

This man turned out to be a so-called friend and neighbor. When our firm was changing hands, the new owners wanted to know who was doing what and this man told the boss *"You don't need him I can do my job and his."* This cost me my job, but I got a job with Mays about a month later. My old boss kept me on because he knew how competent I was. I asked my old friend for a reference since he had taken my job, but he said to me, *"I don't know you."* I was just testing him at the time to see if he was that mean as I gleaned that he was. He eventually died because he was infected with disease caused by working at the same job which he stole from me.

I left the church which I was attending at this time and started going to a church which was closer to home. After staying with this church for over 3 years, the pastor said that the Holy Spirit told him that he should ordain me. But he refused to. One night the assistant pastor was ministering to a woman and she was rebuking witchcraft and other spirits. When she was finished the woman went back to her seat. But the Holy Spirit told me go and administer to her. I went to her and asked if she had gone to the doctor that day and the doctor told her that the baby was in the wrong position. She responded *"Yes! Dr. Waterman. Yes!"* I then asked if I could place my hands on her stomach and she said *"Yes"*. So, I did so and immediately I felt the baby turn. I asked her not to say anything because I did not want to be ostracized. The woman was so happy that she could not keep it for herself. Can you guess what happened after this?

I was told that I should not pray with anymore in the church anymore, that if I wanted to pray I should come in early and pray between 6 - 8 PM. When I asked the Holy Spirit why I was being ostracized for doing as he asked, I was told to go to the church office and I would see why.

I went to the church office and opened the door, there was a group of people praying and when they saw me they froze. I turned away as directed by the Holy Spirit, but I was instructed to slam the door but not to leave and reopen it after a short while. I opened the door again and when they saw me this time they acted as though I was a ghost. It was during that time that I found out that I had the five-fold ministry gifts, and they having observed this also, it was a cause for jealousy.

I was scrutinized to see whether these gifts really dwelt with me. I was approached by one of the seniors at the church and he questioned me as to whether I really had the gifts. He then challenged me by asking me to locate his lost car keys. I asked him if he were playing with me or if he were serious. He then started to say that he was right and I did not have any gifts because I could not tell him where to find his keys. I realized that he had really lost them so I told him where he could find them and he immediately went and got them. When he returned he told me that it was a lucky guess and could I tell him what his wife was praying for. I told him that she was praying for a car, because I decided to play with him a little. He looked at me with a note of triumph and said *"OH, you are wrong because my wife already has a car."* I told him to wait a minute then I told him that she was praying for her sister to get saved. The man turned as red as a ripe cherry, he turned and walked away and never spoke to me again.

One Sunday evening the pastor came in from Kings County where one of the leader's mother was admitted in a serious condition. The pastor got on the pulpit and said everyone should stretch their hands over to the direction of the Kings County Hospital, and in three days she would be out and well because of the power of prayer. I stretched my hands out also but I was told by the Holy Spirit to put my hands down. I began to see things as though they were coming over a large TV screen. I saw the sick woman two grandsons and her daughter, at track 38 Georgia. One of the grandsons had his jacket over his arms and the other had his white shirt opened up. I looked on and I saw the undertakers put the body in the luggage car. The pastor came down and I asked her if I could speak to her. She told me; *"No! No!"* She did not want to hear anything.

About three weeks later I was speaking to one of the grandsons letting him know what I had seen and he told me that he did not know that I was there. I told him when I had seen this. He walked away from me in disbelief. As you can imagine I was ostracized some more, but when anyone was sick I was called to pray for them including their own family. Interesting!

A short while before I left that church; one Sunday when the pastor was about to close the service, a man appeared in front of the pastor. He was dressed with something on his head that looked like a white baker's hat. He had on a white tunic, which came half way up his legs and he had on a pair of sandals that were laced up to his calves. He also had on a blue breast plate that was intermingled with different colors.

He stared at the pastor, and then he came to my right side and stood up. I looked at him and smiled. The pastor noticing me smiling, then he shouted *"WATERMAN what are you smiling at?"* I told him that I was smiling at the man standing at my side. He said *"There is no one beside you."* I then described the person who was standing beside me. He shouted *"Oh my God, that is God's High Priest. In the name of the Father, Son and Holy Ghost everyone get out of my church."*

Accident on My Job

While working on the job at the hospital, I had an accident and was knocked unconscious. When I came to, my supervisor did not allow me to see a doctor. I had bad headaches and an unusual heartbeat. I went to see my family doctor who told me to go at once to the emergency room and I was admitted and put in Intensive Care. I can remember my being there for three days.

At this point the machines, which I was hooked up to, began to go off. The nurse rushed in and when she saw this she said, *"What the @#$% are you doing? If you want to kill him, wait till he gets home; don't kill him on my watch"*

After I got out of the hospital, I was in and out on several occasions because I began to suffer with heart problems. I also began to suffer with severe headaches. Today God has brought me through these problems and I no longer suffer with any of these ailments.

While working for the area hospital, I was asked by one of my supervisors whether I knew how to fix a washing machine because hers was not emptying the water when she washed. I told her that I had worked for Mays, both as an electrical and mechanical engineer, so I would come to her home on my day off, which was Saturday, to see what was wrong with it.

I got to my supervisor's house and began to service the machine. Suddenly, I noticed that she was walking around in her robe, which was unbuttoned. I was distracted by her behavior and had not noticed that I was about to touch live mechanism.

Other Strange Experiences in New York

While I was living at the apartment I had other experiences that were amazing. The Holy Spirit began revealing things to me. On one occasion a neighbor knocked on my door and invited me to her apartment. When I got there, the place smell like rotten eggs, burnt onion skins and other foul smelling things. It really stank. I asked her what had happened and she told me that all she had done was to open a letter she had received from overseas. I told her that she had a visitor, and since I always walked with my Bible, I asked her to open hers and I did the same. We read Psalm 35, 37 & 70, after which I quoted the scripture in Matthew about God giving us the authority over evil spirits. I asked her for a glass of water, and I told her to follow me while I opened the apartment door. I asked her where she wanted the spirit to go if to hell or back to the sender, and she said back to the sender so I did that. Immediately the stench left her apartment.

About three weeks later, I heard a pounding on my door, when I got to the door, there was the woman again, this time she had a letter telling her that the people who sent her the first one had to leave their house and run because it stank. The evil had returned to the sender.

On Friday nights I held a meeting in the living room of the house. A young lady who would go to the G Building every year, because she had lost all of her money which she had invested with a man in a restaurant business. He later claimed that the restaurant was burnt down; and when he received the insurance payment he skipped town leaving her with nothing. I prayed with her and she promised that she would return the following Friday and give her heart to the Lord. She did not keep her word; her friend told me that her baby was ill. I got her phone number and called her and she repeated the same thing. I told her that she should not lie on her child because he would really be sick and I began to describe the young man that was lying in her bed. When I did, I asked if she wanted me to also tell her his name. She screamed, hung the phone up and called me later during the week. I led her to the Lord then; however she would never remain in my presence anymore because she thought that I could read minds. Today she is a qualified RN.

One day I received a call from a woman who told me that she got my number from a friend. I immediately told her that we were being taped to which she replied: *"No! My husband is a mechanic he does not know how to do these things"*. I then described her, and asked her if she was in her bedroom. She was amazed at my accuracy and then I told her that she should not hang up her phone but she should go to her basement and look behind the washing machine under the stairs, there she would see a recorder but she should be careful in removing the wires or she would lose electricity in her house. She did as I had asked and returned to the phone very excited. She asked me where I lived and when I gave her my address she was over in about 20 minutes. When I opened the door she asked if I was Dr. Waterman, I answered "Yes" and she said to me *"Are you an obeah man?"* I said *"Oh, no my dear, the only person I know is Jesus Christ, who is my Lord and Savior"*. I asked her to come in and I told her what she wanted to tell me about her house and I advised her, what to do. Because of my advice, she was able to avoid foreclosure, but she lost a lot of money too, because she did not listen to some of my advice. I would call her and I could tell her exactly where she was and what she was wearing or doing. She became fascinated with this and I became caught up in using my gift for personal reasons.

At a church, the pastor was praying for me because I was sweating profusely. I heard him praying about diabetes and other things rebuking them in Jesus' name. When I got home I had a meal, something to drink and went to bed. At around 7:30 pm I was awakened and had to go to the hospital. When I got there the nurse examined me and was about to send me home. She asked me if I ever had a finger stick. I asked her what that was and she explained about being something used to check blood sugar. She then pricked my finger and checked it. The results were so astonishing that she assumed that the machine was broken. She did this 3 times. The third time she grabbed me by the neck and ran with me to ICU. She told the doctor that my sugar was 810. The doctor said that was impossible or I would be dead. She said that she checked it 3 times. The doctor told her to give me some insulin which she did.

During the night a bed became available and when I got to the room, the man across the room said to me: *"Man that bed is still warm from the man who died there." I refused to get* in the bed immediately, but the nurse said that I had a bad reaction to the insulin and should get in bed. I asked her to let me pray first because of the news I was greeted with. She allowed me and I became courageous, I had a good night's sleep.

My medication was changed and I was discharged a few days later. I had been given a new medication for the blood pressure, which I also had a bad reaction to. I was walking the dog and felt a burning sensation on my tongue. There was a nurse visiting at the time, and I asked her to check my tongue where it was burning. She told me that it was nothing but she would take me to the hospital so that they could put something on it to help me.

When I got to the hospital, I thought it a little strange that she went directly to the head nurse instead of taking me to register. The nurse told me to follow her and they put me on a stretcher and took me to the ICU once again. About three hours later, I was completely swollen from head to toe. I tried to turn my head to look up to heaven, but could not do so. I said in my mind, "Are you going to let him do this to me again?" At that moment I returned to a state of normalcy.

I called in the doctors and asked that I be sent home. The doctors said to me, "No Mr. Waterman, you are completely swollen and we are going to put in a tube so that you could breathe." I said "No doctor, nothing is wrong with me anymore, check me." They checked me all over and began to back away from me. They found nothing but sent me home telling my family that if I should begin to swell again I should be rushed into the hospital. It was however a miracle, I went home and there was no swelling, no need for anyone to rush me to the hospital.

Sometime after this incident, I got up early in the morning and had a cup of tea. I took my blood pressure medication and after talking with relatives for a while, I was still feeling tired so I went back to sleep. About 2 to 3 hours later I woke up and forgetting that I had already taken my medication, I took it again. I was sitting at the kitchen table talking with relatives, and I promptly passed out. When I came to I heard my niece rebuking the spirit of death and praying for God to restore me to good health.

My family called 911. When the paramedics got there and checked my blood pressure, it was 50/46. They strapped me to the stretcher and took me to the emergency, and because I was so out of, it they also put an IV into my arm on the way there.

When I got to the hospital they ran all types of tests, refusing to believe what I had told them. A couple of days later, a Caucasian doctor came to me in the afternoon with a pill for me and told me that he was going to keep me one more day. A nurse was standing behind him and frantically waving her hand from side to side, was lisping to me *"Don't take it, don't take it."* I was thinking how unusual it was for a doctor to be giving me a pill and water so I listened to the nurse. I put the pill under my tongue and drank the water and he left. The nurse came to me and said *"Did you take that pill?"* I said *"No"* and I took it out of my mouth and held it in my hands. She said *"You just saved your damn life!"* About 2 am, I felt as though my head was coming off. I had only had the pill under my tongue for about three seconds. When I complained to the nurse, she told me to find the doctor and tell him how I felt.

I swiftly walked to the doctor's lounge and found him. As I approached he saw me, and believe me, he turned as white as a sheet. When I explained to him how I felt, he told me that the pill was working and that he would come and check me at 6am. I never saw him again. I was discharged that very day by another doctor.

I finally moved away from this couple and I went to live in a room of a church that I attended and was an associate pastor.

Living at the Church

While living at the Church, one of my roommates asked me to do him a favor. He said that he and his wife, who was an Indian woman decided to separate and he was doing his divorce himself. He asked me to give the divorce paper to his wife for him because the law said that he could not serve her himself. I asked him if there were any problems between himself and his wife and he said "no" and that she was living with her boyfriend and all was fine.

One morning he called me and said *"Doc, she is out there, just give this to her please."* I put on a dressing gown and went downstairs and opened the door and gave it to her as he had requested. She responded *"You! I will fix you!"* I returned to my room and did not think anything of it again until about three weeks later.

I went to the stove to make some oatmeal and tea, but before I could turn on the stove I realized that my dressing gown was on fire. I quickly untied the robe, let it drop to the floor and proceeded to stamp out the flames. The fire came about all by itself. I told my sister about the incident and she was convinced that I was making it up until her son, who was also married to an Indian woman had the same experience. Wow! The plans of the enemy of our souls come in many ways. We must beware!

Journey to the Celestial

The pastor of the church I was attended asked us to fast for three days. At the end of the third day she told me that God had told her that I had to go on for another 4 days. I had no arguments with God's instructions so I went home and went into my bed to continue my fast. I was told to get out of the bed and lie on the floor. I asked to take a sheet with me as I lay on the floor amidst the cockroaches. I could feel them crawl over me at times, but I was not concerned. When I had fasted for about five days, I felt the presence of someone come through the unopened door. I felt as if he/she came over me and began to massage my tummy. I then became aware of the fact that was out of my body. I felt as though my hand was taken and I began to rise in the air above everything. I could see the earth getting smaller and smaller beneath me. I remember thinking how beautiful it looked and how much it reminded me of a marble, a beautiful blue marble.

Next, I remember passing Saturn. It looked like the color of toffee and off white, and had flat rings around it. What fascinated me most were the 2 or 3 smaller planets that were going around it together with the rings. We picked up speed and the next place we all were was on a manicured lawn. In the distance I saw a beautiful city with bright white lights gleaming from it. When my eyes became adjusted to it I became aware of its awesome and indescribable beauty. Although I was not taken into the city, I was shown a beautiful mansion, with steps on either side where people were entering. I saw them close up as though I was looking at them through a magnifying glass. I could see details of their faces, such as moles and hairs.

While looking at this awesome sight I began to walk into a river that got deeper and deeper as I walked. I heard myself think *"What is this?"* and immediately I heard an answer. *"The Water of Life"* again I heard myself *"Can I drink?"* and I heard the answer *"You are standing in it."* I did not consume. I looked on, and I saw little buds of flowers falling into the water and floating past me.

After sometime I found myself sitting in a military vehicle and the officer who was escorting me had a thin leather strap across his shoulders. He also wore a large leather belt. After driving for a while he stopped and motioned for me to get out. He told me to wait there for instructions. I then heard a thump and became aware that I was back in my own body. I was horrified because I so enjoyed where I was I did not want to come back. Out of Body Experiences are amazing!

On the final day of the fast, I was told to pray every hour. After praying on the hour I saw three chairs come down over the bed and I was asked what I wished for. I said *"To know you better."* I was told that it would be granted to me with more. I did not know exactly what more I was to expect.

On one occasion, when I was suffering with enlarged prostate, it began to bleed. I called a relative over, and he drove me to the hospital. When I was admitted they immediately operated on me and when I came out of the anesthesia the doctor told me that everything went well. The operation lasted for about an hour. Meanwhile my relative was waiting on me in the waiting room. I needed to go to the bathroom and the nurse asked me if I would like her to come with me because I may likely have a lot of pain and there would be some blood. In my machismo, I told her *"No."* I thought that I was very able, since I considered myself grown. She asked if I was sure, and I indicated that I was. When I got to the bathroom and felt the pain and saw the blood I screamed so loudly that my relative heard me from the waiting room. When I returned to the nurse she asked me for my relative because *I was* about to be discharged. I looked for him but could not find him, so I told her that he was downstairs. She discharged me and since I could not find him anywhere I called a taxi and went home by myself.

About an hour later I heard the door bell ring, and when I went to answer it, I found my relative at the door. I asked him what had happened and he said that he had heard me scream from where he was and that he could not take it so he left the hospital.

Guidance from Above

When I worked in Manhattan at a carbon producing firm, my pay was very small so I was entitled to food stamps. One day when I went for the food stamps, I was told by the clerk that I could not get any stamps because the files were out of order and scattered on the floor and the window sills and she could not look through them to locate mine. I asked her if I could get it for her without touching any other if she would give it to me. She said yes, but you are crazy and I would also have to call security. I again told her that I would not touch another file but my own. She said: ""*Let's see you do that*". I went straight to my file and picked it out without touching another one. Her eyes were opened widely as I handed her the file and she saw that it was indeed mine. She looked at me very puzzled as she said, "*How the %$@# did you do that?*" I said that I am a Christian. She said, "*Who are you?*" I gave her an explanation about my experience.

Later, I felt very sorry that I did not give the glory to God and to the Holy Spirit. I went before him in tears and pleaded for his forgiveness. As I was kneeling there, I felt as if someone had rested their hand on my shoulder. I stopped praying and looked around to see who it was, but I was the only person there. Then I knew that I was forgiven and I got up and went upstairs with a peaceful heart.

Recognizing a Pattern

Again, "*Gifts are given to men without repentance*" so says Corinthians. Therefore I began to take my gifts seriously unlike when I was 3, 5, and 7 years of age. I have since learned to value the occurrence of the supernatural which started with my childhood visions. There is no one who can shut me up when I have a message from the Holy Spirit. I have learned to take them seriously every time whether anyone believes me or not. I have come to know God for myself.

There came a day when I was in England, that I dreamt that someone had shot me in the head, but I would be okay. When I got to work, out of the blue, I decided to tell the dream to someone. I chose to tell it to a white guy, who insulted me in the worst way. He told me to get my black so and so out of there. I protested that it was only a dream, and that I could tell it to any of the five hundred people around but for some reason I chose him. He again rebuked me and I left.

The next day, as I was on my way I noticed him approaching me and decided to turn around and go in the other direction. He called after me and I told him that I was not up for any confrontation that day. He asked me to wait. As I turned to face him, I noticed that his eyes were all teary and red. I asked him what the matter was. He then told me that when he got home the evening before, he received a telegram from the British Home Office telling him that his brother was shot in the head and he would be O.K. He told me that he immediately remembered our conversation, and recognized that God was preparing him for the telegram. He also said that I had a gift and I should use it wisely. Amen

During the time that I stayed in England, there were attacks made on some stores by persons who had the intention of burning and blowing up those stores. This happened in the Irish Republic and the mainland. At that time no one could tell how they were accomplishing those events. I, however, dreamt that it was done by persons entering a store with a lighted cigarette and putting it together with a book of matches into a coat pocket or some other place where it would easily be ignited, and leave without being detected. I had vivid images of how this was done.

One day while I was praying over the phone with a prophet, I felt a big bang in my head, I saw fire descending from heaven and two extra large palms of hands stretched out over the area. The hands proceeded to take a Tartan rug and place it over the whole scene. I asked her what was the interpretation and she told me that a disaster over Scotland was imminent. When she told me this it was Saturday night. On Monday morning there was news of a plane being bombed in mid air and the scene was the same as I had envisioned. It was like déjà vu, to me.

Another time I was asleep and dreaming that I was in a theatre, looking at a screen. On the screen I saw helicopters and soldiers taking off from Barbados and landing in an Island which I recognized as a Caribbean Island. I saw them surround a place and take out some Caucasian girls and boys, put them on a truck and escorted them to what looked like an airport. I watched the whole event where the marines found very little resistance from the country which had been overtake within hours. When I saw the events of the Grenada take over by the US in the news, it was like déjà vu, again.

I moved to Ebertsfield, Brooklyn New York after I left the Church building. I got an apartment on the 11th floor and while I was getting it ready for me to move in, a woman came and opened the door and began to look around. She had not said a word to neither me nor the man who was helping me get things ready. When she was satisfied, she went out again.

A couple of weeks later I heard a knock on the door, without opening it I asked *"Who is it?"* and I heard the response *"I am the owner of this apartment."* I asked him how could I help him and he told me that the Post Office supervisor told him that I received a parcel for him. I said to him "Sir, I don't know you. *"Why would I be receiving your package?"* He then said "We'll see, I will fix you" then he left. I had no idea who this man was until one of my neighbors said to me *"Oh I see that you live in the Obeah man's apartment"* I paid no attention to him until one morning I got up to find a beautiful young lady lying in bed beside me. I looked up at my door and saw that it was locked and chained. I knew that I had not let anyone into my apartment so I jumped over her and went and got my bottle of holy water and started sprinkling it on her. She went *'poof,* and disappeared.

A week later, a friend and her daughter came to visit, and while he daughter was on the computer, I was sitting in a plastic chair reading a book. The plastic chair, on which I was sitting, suddenly had its two front legs broken off and thrown in front of me on the floor. I got off the chair and said *"Is that the best you can do?"* I prayed and later went to bed and in the middle of my sleep found myself awakened by the shower which was not on. I got up and went to the bathroom and *I* saw evidence that someone had taken a bath. There was water on the floor as though someone had stepped out after their bath. I looked at the situation and I said *"In the name of Jesus, you will not shower in here again, don't you ever touch my shower again, now get out!"*

The following day as I was praying in the apartment alone, I noticed about a dozen length of hairs which were about 10 to 14" long appeared on my thighs. I took them up and threw them into the garbage and I said. *"Is this the best you can do? I pay the rent in here and I would be leaving when I am good and ready."*

One Sunday While I was visiting a local church on Church Avenue, Brooklyn, I went in and noticed a beautiful young lady with gorgeous eyes. I kept staring at her instead of paying attention to the service. I decided then that I would have to get her telephone number, so I approached her at the end of the service and told her how I felt. She told me that she would give me the number, but I had to first meet her mother and she gave me her mother's address. When I got to her mother, she asked me my name and when I told her she asked if I had any family in Trinidad and I told her yes and explained as far as I knew where they lived and their circumstances. I called names of my father's sisters whom I knew to be Martha and Joanne. She said to me Martha Waterman; I said *"Yes"*. She then said to me *"That is my mother."* At this point we both started laughing, then we hugged each other and since then we have been living as close family, as we ought.

One day a woman who attended church with me came to me saying that her son was arrested and his father, who was a police officer had gone down to the jail to make arrangements for his release. Although he was told that he would be released, the woman who had him arrested now identified him as the person who had stolen some items from her so he was taken to court instead of being released.

I prayed with her and asked her if she was paying her tithes, and she said *"Yes"*. So I told her that she had favor from God, which meant that she had an unfair advantage over anyone else. I told her to go down to the court and get her son. When the case was called the witness did not appear and so the case was thrown out, and her son was released. I told her to get her son out of that area. He later began attending school in Manhattan, and became a very outstanding student. Praise God!

A few weeks later she called me again and told me that he was arrested again. His explanation was that he was walking to the subway with this young lady who was smoking a joint and an undercover policeman walked towards them and took out his ID the young lady then handed the joint to him. I prayed with her again and I asked her if she believed him and she said no. I then asked her if God had given her favor before and she said yes. So I told her that he can do it again. When she went to court that Monday, there was a senior and also a junior judge who was in training. The junior judge wanted to give him a year in jail, but the senior judge called him and looked into his eyes and said, *"Young man, if I catch you in my court again I would throw the book at you, go on home."* I began to mentor him and he was able to pass his exams for Kingsbrook College. I invited them to my church, and a visiting prophetess told him that God had called him to the ministry.

After leaving Ebertsfield I moved to a one bedroom apartment at New York Avenue., and I attended a church called Jehovah Tsidkenu. From time to time I would teach and preach at the Church. There were two churches, one was in the Bronx and the other was in Brooklyn. The pastor asked me to take over the church while she was on outreach in the West Indies.

After church was over in the Bronx, we had to take the Brooklyn Queens Expressway (BQE) to get home, which passed through a cemetery.

One night while we were traveling along the road, I noticed a Chinese man wearing white shirt, and black trousers. He was walking ahead of us directly in the part of the car. I became alarmed as to why he would be putting himself in such danger. Then I noticed that he had no feet. I remained silent because I recognized that he had to be a ghostly figure. The car went right through him. I then asked the driver if she saw him and she asked where he was. I told her that she had just passed through him. She became concerned and tried to stop the car. I then told her that it was not a physical person, so she should not fear.

On another occasion I saw a Jewish young man, wearing a black felt hat. He was standing in the cemetery with a book in his hand bowing as if in prayer. I asked those in the car if they saw him and only one of them saw what I had seen. But she did not know what he was a ghost until I pointed it out. That reminded me of when I was in the Caribbean and I saw things, when I told my mother she would shut me up.

While I was at that church, a good friend called me and told me that she had cervical cancer. I told her to place her hands over herself and I prayed for her. Then I told her to go back to the doctor and ask for another examination. This time it was negative. Around the same time a close family relative called me saying that she had lumps in both breasts, I told her to place her hands over herself and I prayed for her and the lumps disappeared. With these two individuals, the enemy brought back the cancer about twelve years later. Had they read Nahum 1:9, *"What do you imagine against the Lord? He would make an utter end: affliction shall not rise up the second time."* Both went ahead and have both their breasts removed and they also had hysterectomy done.

I was told to call a relative by her brother, and I asked her, what was the urgency in calling her? She replied that she was a cancer survivor. It was revealed to me at that time that her left breast was missing. I asked her what had happened to her breast and she hung up the phone on me. About 3 months later she called me crying because she was taking chemo and radiation. She complained about boils on her private parts, and she did not want to live anymore. I asked her to stop crying and place her hands over the boils. I had not heard from her for some time until a friend asked me to call her. He mentioned the possibility of our closeness since her healing from the boils immediately after my praying for her. This was how I knew what had happened for she had not told me herself. May God bless her, regardless!

I was introduced to a young pastor who was in a very bad relationship. A few weeks later he came to me and asked if I would accompany him to a police station in a Brooklyn community. While we were traveling in the car he shared with me that his wife had broken his wrist by throwing a VCR at him and had tried several times to have him arrested. He feared that he would be arrested this time for trying to see the kids without her permission. When we got to the station we began to talk about the scriptures and the goodness of God. The detective came in and asked him to accompany her, while I had to wait. The detective came back and told me to come and say goodbye to my friend. I followed her and when we got to him he was in handcuffs. I hugged him and told him that he was not going to prison but that he was being sent on assignment. His assignment was to lead three people he was going to meet there, to Christ. He pushed me away and muttered something about me being crazy. The detective showed me how to get the bus, and I went home.

The following day I received a call from the young man. He was excited as he told me that I would not believe what had happened to him. He related to me how everyone except him was called the night before. He then sat on the bench by himself when a man came over and asked if he was a pastor and when he answered yes he asked him to pray for him, and he did. When that man left, another man came over and explained that the man he had prayed for and himself were in a fight over his wife, and they were both arrested. He asked that he also be prayed for. A third man who was observing came over and asked that he also be prayed for. He said that at this point he remembered what I had said, so when he saw another man coming his way he stretched out his hand and said *""Just touch my hand and everything would be all right."* But the man did not want anything to do with him. At this point I asked him *"What part of 3 people did you not understand?"* He then told me that they began taking him up the stairs when suddenly they stopped and took off his handcuffs and told him that they did not have enough evidence to take him before the judge so he could go home. He told me that when I had hugged him and told him of his assignment that he wanted to smack me. He thought that I was really going off the deep end at that time.

I was invited to preach at a Seventh day Adventist Church. That Saturday morning we marched in our doctorial robes, and when we got to the podium, I was introduced to the congregation and the pastor sat down. I took the pulpit, and I immediately received a word of knowledge. I was told to tell a young boy in the front seat, that God will now cure him of sickle cell disease. I told God that I would do it when I was finished preaching. I heard a thunderous, "What?" I lifted my hands in the air as I said *"Oh God forgive me! I did not realize who I was talking to".* Immediately the Pastor and his attendant rushed to me and asked me to sit down. I told them that I was okay, and that I had received a word from God. They again tried to get me to sit down. I told them to take it easy and listen to what I had to say. I told the young man that God will heal him at that moment from sickle cell. He got up and went over to his mother with tears in his eyes and said *"Why did you tell him that I had sickle cell?"* she replied, *"I have never seen this man in my life."* The pastor was so upset that he left the church afterwards without even speaking to me.

Later in the week, the pastor called me and said, *"This is not my request, the church members are requesting that you come back"* I said *"I am not coming back there, you left me in the lurch, hungry and with only enough fare to catch the bus."* He then told me that he would give me something for both times if I should return.

On my return, I preached first, and then I had an altar call. While I was praying for the people, God told me that a certain woman who is in front of you now, all she wants is $1, 000. I told her and he began to laugh. I told her what God had said, and she said *"Yes! Yes! Yes! That is all I want."* I said to her, *"Miss, He is right in front of me, ask him for more."* She said *"No".* I then told her that by Nov 6th, she would have her $1000, as God had shown to me.

On Nov 6th, she called me and told me that she got the money and she asked her pastor if this was of God. She said he told her to call me and give me $100. This woman came to me with a proposition for an entry in a magazine and I told her that she should take the $50 cost from the $100 that she had for me. She said that is not the way she does business, that I had to pay her the $50 and on her return she would give me the $100. When she came back with the magazine she gave it to me saying, *"I don't owe you a dime."* I responded, *"And I don't sell God's gift either."*

In 2007 I began to pass blood in my stool. I at once contacted a doctor who asked me to see a specialist. The specialist called me in and a colonoscopy was done. The result was that I had cancer of the pancreas, rectum and anus. This was surprising to me because I had done a colonoscopy just the year before and it was negative. This specialist introduced me to another specialist whom he said was his good friend. After examining me he told me that there was no cancer in my liver, because it felt smooth, and there was no cancer in my neck and since he had 27 years of experience he was sure that even if there was cancer, there would not be much invasive surgery, just a little tummy tuck.

I went for 3 other examinations where he used a scope on me and he told me that he had not seen any cancer in my pancreas; but he saw in the rectum and anus. My friends at three churches when they heard of my predicament prayed for me and told me that there was nothing there anymore. I had the greatest confidence in my doctor however, who was preaching to me better than any of my pastors. He told me that he was guided by god and of his belief in him. To be on the safe side I decided to allow him to do exploratory surgery on me because I had been a little doubtful of all the things that had been going on.

When I went in for the surgery it was supposed to take me about 2 hours according to the doctor. My wife told me that it took all day, and that they wheeled me into ICU with all types of tubes attached to me and that there was a code blue while I was in the operation room. The following day I remembered the nurse waking me and asking if I was OK. I opened my eyes and I asked her what had happened. She told me that I had surgery, and that it was touch and go. A little later my wife and daughter came in and my wife began to relate things to me that I had no idea of.

My wife said that on my way back to ICU, I raised myself up and gave her a thumbs up. I don't even know how that was possible and I have no recollection of it. While she was talking to me a doctor came in. He came over to me and said "Oh my goodness, you are Waterman, you are my patient. He said this because I had been his patient for sometime in an unrelated case. He then told me that he answered the code blue, and that everything was OK with me and that I should come in to see him in 4 weeks time when I was healed.

The doctor who did the surgery came to me about 3 days later. I asked him why he had to cut me so far up in the abdomen almost to my chest. He told me that he had to see my liver. I told him that he had ensured me that my liver was OK. He said it again in a very matter of fact way and he left. While I was in ICU I was losing so much blood because I was cut so far up that I had to be given blood. I received 2 pints of blood. I asked that they not give me a third pint but that I should be given the necessary things that would boost the blood level. They agreed and I was given what?

On the fifth day after the surgery, my dressing was removed. I was alarmed to see how high the cut had been in my chest and petrified to see that the wound was still open. I began to pray and ask God why this had happened to me. God asked me if I had asked the doctor which God he was talking about when he mentioned God to me. By this time I was stable enough to be moved to a ward. When I arrived at the ward, I heard the groans of a man who was next to me with the curtains drawn. I was told by the Holy Spirit that I should say to that man "Lift your hands in the air and say Jesus three times, and you both would walk out of here tonight." I then asked "Lord what is wrong with him." I was told that his small intestines were twisted, and that I should do as I was ordered to.

Immediately I heard *"You are going to tell him what? You have 3 IV's going, a morphine pump in your hand for the pain, and your legs wrapped, to help your circulation"* At this point I hesitated. His doctors came in and wheeled him out before I could have a chance to speak to him. They took him for a catscan and when the results came in they told him that his small intestines were twisted and they were taking him to the operating room. I felt very ashamed to think that I doubted God again. God spoke to me again however telling me that it was OK and that I would be out of there by Saturday which was three days away.

When I got home I had a visiting nurse who told me that I was healing so fast, that in her experience she had never seen anything like it, and asked me what I was using. After two months she told me to go and see the doctor and let him see this and there was no need for her to come to my home anymore. When I went to see the doctor, he himself was surprised by my recovery and stated that I should not be healing that fast.

There came the time when I had to see the doctor who helped to revive me, and who had asked me to come to see him. When I got there he proceeded to examine me as usual. When I told him that he could not examine my prostate in the usual way he said *"Of course I can, everything was OK, I was there."* And he tried to, but found out that he could not because my rectum and anus had been removed. He shouted "Damn!" then he snatched off his gloves threw them in the bin and walked out without saying another word. He sent in his nurse for me to get dressed and give me another date. He made arrangements for me to see another doctor. Because of these circumstances, I refused to have chemotherapy and radiation, and it has now been 1 yr and 8 months and all blood test, catscan and colonoscopy have been normal.

Be Silent in the Church No More

One Thursday night I brought the word and after I was finished preaching, I received a word of knowledge for one of the sisters who had already received a word from the prophetess. I was told to let her know that she was going to get her miracle that same night. I had not even remembered telling her that it was she who told me. That same night when she got home she received a call from the hospital telling her that a kidney was available for her.

We had a Pre-Father's Day dinner at the church hall, and as soon as they were about to announce the winner of the ticket, I received a word of knowledge as to who would receive it. I hesitated to say anything except to my wife. Low and behold it was just whom I had been told. I had forgotten that when God shows up he also shows off.

One Sunday we had another prophetess in the house, and a visiting Pastor. The organist, who was a young Caucasian man, was about to travel to Europe. The Spirit of the Lord asked me to go over and minister to him. I said to him *"I understand that you are traveling, would you be going anywhere near Budapest and would you be anywhere near Prague?"* He said *"Yes, that is exactly where I am staying."* I told him that the spirit of God would be with him and he would be protected and return safely. I then left him with an astonished look on his face.

Being Used Prophetically

There was this lady who called me from Florida. She said that she was finding life to be difficult at the time because she had no job. I remember looking at the clock and it was 11.59 pm. I received a word for her at that moment and I told her not to worry because she would get a job right away. She then asked me *"How could that be so at 12 midnight?"* At that moment she received another call and asked me to hold on, while she answer that call. I found myself holding for about 10 minutes and when she had not returned I hung up the phone. About three months later, she called me to tell me that the person on the other line was her friend who had called her in to work for her right away and told her she could keep the job. She thought, at that time, that she would have to give me something so she did not call me back, and the job had lasted for three months. I told her that her train of thought was not wise and that I would have prayed for her to have a job indefinitely and in any case I do not sell God's gift.

That same lady called me about three months ago and told me that she was having some problems with her house and the insurance company was not paying for the cost of repair. I prayed with her again and asked her what amount she would consider to be fair to ask God for. Would it be $250,000, $500,000, or $20,000 She told me that if she got $20,000 she would be happy. I told her that we would touch and agree for God to give her $20,000. About 3 weeks later she called me and told me that she received a check for $1,030.00 and another check for $20,000 exactly. She then asked me for my address so that she could bless me. She asked me to pray with her again so that she can believe God for $500,000. To this day I have not heard from her again; nor did I receive her promised gift.

There was another lady who called me because she was about to be evicted. I prayed with her and on my way out I saw a New York Lotto form so I took it up, filled it out and gave it to her. I have not heard from her for about a month so I went to visit her and found her moving out. So I said to her *"Thank God, what happened, how would you make out?"* She told me that the Lotto form which I had filled out for her she only got 5 numbers on it and she would not be able to give me anything because she did not get the 6 numbers. I have not heard from her since then.

Another sister had a house in Brooklyn and she asked me to run the house for her. I had picked up the rent and sent it to her the first month that was assigned. One day I saw someone from the gas company who came to cut off the gas because she owed $489.73. Since I was now taking care of the house for her I decided to pay off the bill for her. I called her and told her that I had paid the bill and that she owed me for taking care of the building and also for paying the bill. She told me that she had not asked me to do that so she did not owe me anything. I had to take this woman to court and although the court ordered her to pay, she still did not. She has since sold the house and left the neighborhood.

I was approached by a family member whose son was detained in prison because of his drug use. I looked at him and I told him that he did not only use marijuana but he also uses crack cocaine. He vehemently denied this. I asked him if he remembered a piece of crack falling on his leg and burning him that same week. He again denied any use. I then asked him if he had been in prison and he said yes. I told him that he had been given a sandwich by the guard and a box of milk on the Thursday night for dinner, which he didn't even eat because it was taken from him by one of the prisoners. He replied "Yes!" Then I said to him *"If God knows what you had for dinner a week ago, don't you think he knows what you did yesterday?"* He bent his head then and had nothing to say.

One day one of my church friends, whom I will call ID, told me that she had a dream and the name of a young man with whom she was talking was written across her bed head. I asked God for the interpretation of the dream and I told her that she should be careful because that young man had the HIV virus. A day later I got a word from the Lord to call her and let her know that the other man whom she had not mentioned was also HIV positive. About six months later it was confirmed that they both had the virus.

She wanted to know how I had known about the second guy when she had not even mentioned him. I let her know that she had asked me to pray for her and therefore God had revealed it to me. She then told me that she had stayed away from me for some time for fear that I would read her mind.

For some time I had been praying for a sister because her house was about to go into foreclosure. After attending church on a Thursday, she called me and told me that from the message given at the church she had a positive feeling that something was going to happen. She again called me the next Monday to let me know that she had received a letter from the bank advising her that her mortgage was reduced considerably. This had happened after we had prayed to the Lord for his intervention, because she had been turned down three times before, when she applied for a reduction.

Inventions

When I came from England to the United States of America, I was a qualified Flight Instructor. While I was working for a local hospital in Brooklyn, I was given a car to keep for the bishop, whose church I was affiliated with. I parked it in front of the hospital one day and tried to start the car but it would not start. Someone nearby said to me "You'd better check for your battery." I got out and looked under the hood and there was no battery. I had to replace this battery and I decided to put a car alarm on the car.

After all the drawings I paid a Patent company $8,000.00 to submit my car alarm drawings for USA Patent, for Royalties or for Permanent sale. Sometime later, I returned to the building only to find that they had disappeared. I contacted a patent lawyer who submitted the patent a year later. The patent was granted 3 years later without any explanation about the delay.

I received a check from the FCC stating that they had raided the company that I submitted my work to, because they had changed their address 3 times. In all I received 2 checks from the FCC the total amounts not even close to what I had paid to have the car alarm patented. They had found out that my work was stolen by these people and being used as if it were their own.

I had filed at that time was for an alarm system for an automobile. I filed this in October 1987 and received the Patent in Feb 1990 CAR ALARM Patent No. US 4,901,054. It was "A computerized alarm system for an automobile, which is also capable of rendering the vehicle useless to anyone making a forced entry, is disclosed. The invention includes a computer panel which is equipped with a keyboard of entering a secret code. The alarm system of the present invention further includes a voice synthesizer which verbally warns intruders not to take further action; in an attempt to deter theft or vandalism."

There is neither an American nor foreign company, which has had a patent like this before this.

I had also filed for an Airplane Security System Patent in July of 2002. I received the Patent in February of 2004. It was an airplane security system particularly for a commercial airliner to thwart any possible hijacking actions. It included an on-board device for allowing a person not on-board the airplane to override an on-board piloting system for the airplane. This on-board device is used together with an off-board device for allowing the person not on-board the plane to contact the on-board device for overriding the on-board piloting system. The security person can then utilize a device for directing a flight path for the airplane that would differ from the flight path originally intended by those on-board and piloting the airplane. This also includes providing for the safe landing of the airplane.

I had given power of attorney to a patent lawyer in Chicago. He approached Boeing Aircraft for me and I was assigned a lawyer who emailed me twice and then I could not reach him again. I have since noticed that Boeing has licensed 2 aircraft makers, one European and one American to develop my invention and I have been left out in the cold. AIRPLANE SECURITY SYSTEM Patent No. US 6,691,956 B1

I filed a Patent for a Computer Assisted Danger Alarm with Emergency Braking System in July of 2004. I received the Patent in June of 2006. It was "A computer assisted early warning and emergency braking system for a vehicle is disclosed. The computer system responds to abnormal tire and/or road sensor data by generating a signal which activates the horn, thereby alerting the driver that the vehicle is in an unsafe condition. The computer may commence rapid braking in order to avoid a dangerous situation if appropriate driver corrections do not occur in a timely fashion. Therefore, the present invention provides an increased margin of safety, particularly when the vehicle is traveling at higher speeds. The present invention can also alert others when a driver is not responding with appropriate corrective action, such as might be the case during sickness. Examples include: slumping over the steering wheel due to a heart attack, and or being asleep at the wheel, etc. In the case of a false alarm, the driver can inactivate the system by manual activation of the vehicle horn. In the case of a non-responsive driver, the option for the activation of an emergency locator system can be included."

I have now noticed that one of the famous car manufacturers have the device and the complete invention on their cars. Again I have been left out in the rain. COMPUTER ASSISTED DANGER ALARM WITH EMERGENCY BRAKING SYSTEM Patent No. US 7, 061,374 B2

I now have 6 Certificates of Registration waiting to be Patented. It has been a real struggle for me. God has given me the wisdom to do these things. These inventions I recognize have been his doing; but for whatever reason they have been stolen from me. Yet God is persisting in revealing things to me, and more and more inventions. I hope that I have learnt enough from the past so that the mistakes I have made with these inventions are not repeated. I still hope I will have the opportunity to reap the blessings from knowledge/inventions which He has given to me.

I was at a local church in Brooklyn at one time and we had set up a prosperity table. I took the copper plaque that I had received for the Car Alarm System, and put it on the prosperity table. It was on show for about a week, the following Sunday as my foot passed the thresh-hold of the church the Holy Spirit told me to go downstairs and look in the garbage, and recover my Plaque.

On my way down one of the prophetess handed me red cloth to wave, to my surprise the plaque was sticking out of the garbage ready to be dumped. I wrapped the Plaque in the red cloth and I had a word of knowledge, I was told "Serville, I am not finished with this as yet, take it home." Only one person questioned what I was doing, and I told her months later what had transpired, as for anyone else they had no clue that I had retrieved my property.

And to this day, I have no idea who was responsible, but I resigned from that church the following Sunday.

Conclusion

In the conclusion of these colourful incidents and stories of my life, one would ask God *"Why?"* But the answer is *"Why not?"* I think that if nothing happens to you, God has no reason to show up, and to show off. Remember, in Psalm 23, He said that he would prepare a table before you in the presence of your enemies. When God shows up in my situation my cup must run over. I believe that it is my time. As Job puts it, *"Though he slay me, yet will I trust him"* and he concluded *"I shall wait until my change comes."*

The conclusion of one's experience is not the end of all, but the beginning of God's showing up in one's life.

Money is not the root of all evil. Money is to be circulated and not hoarded. Those who have stolen my inventions; there is a saying, "What goes around comes around." I know that God has a hand in the affairs of my life. Sometimes I have asked Him *"Lord when would you intervene in my behalf?"* and the answer is simple, God does not come when I think he should, but He is always on time.

There is a quotation from the philosopher Socrates *"When a man marries a good wife, he is a contented man, but when a man marries a bad wife, he becomes a philosopher."* I now hold a Doctorate in Divinity, and a PhD. in Philosophy, majored in Theology from the International Theological Seminary of California. I have proven my point. The God we serve is a consuming fire. This quotation from Isaiah 43:1-3 *"But now thus saith the LORD that created thee, O Jacob, and he that formed thee, O Israel, fear not, for I have redeemed thee, have called thee by thy name; thou art mine. When thou passeth through the waters I will be with thee; and through the rivers, they shall not overflow thee; when thou walkest through the fire, thou shalt not be burned; neither shall the flame kindle upon thee. For I am the LORD thy God, the Holy One of Israel, thy Savior. I gave Egypt for thy ransom,*

Ethiopia and Seba for thee". Matthew 19:29 states: *"And every one that hath forsaken houses, or brethren or sisters, or father or mother or wife or children or lands for my names sake, shall receive a hundredfold and shall inherit everlasting life"*. Jesus said *"Heaven and earth shall pass away before one jot of my word should fall to the ground."*

Finally, in concluding this book, (Hope springs eternal). I have enclosed authentic photographs and scans of documents as proof for the readers' enjoyment.

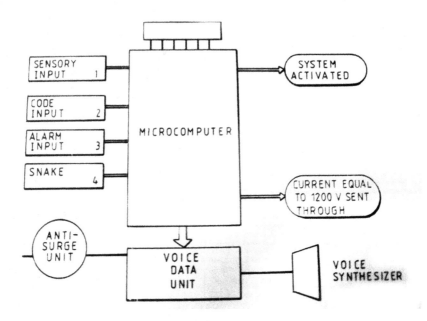

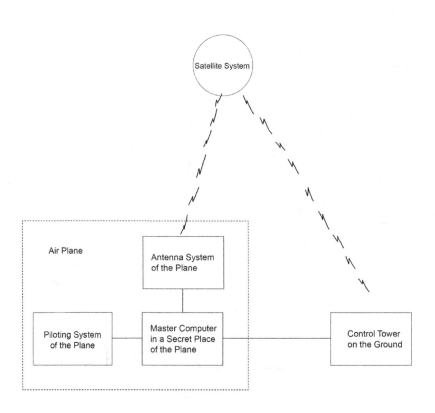

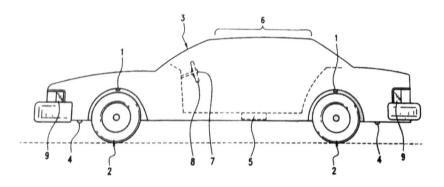

Printed in the United States
by Baker & Taylor Publisher Services